The Future

THIS EDITION
Editorial Management by Oriel Square
Produced for DK by WonderLab Group LLC
Jennifer Emmett, Erica Green, Kate Hale, *Founders*

Editors Grace Hill Smith, Libby Romero, Maya Myers, Michaela Weglinski;
Photography Editors Kelley Miller, Annette Kiesow, Nicole DiMella; **Managing Editor** Rachel Houghton;
Designers Project Design Company; **Researcher** Michelle Harris; **Copy Editor** Lori Merritt;
Indexer Connie Binder; **Proofreader** Larry Shea; **Reading Specialist** Dr. Jennifer Albro;
Curriculum Specialist Elaine Larson

Published in the United States by DK Publishing
1745 Broadway, 20th Floor, New York, NY 10019

Copyright © 2023 Dorling Kindersley Limited
DK, a Division of Penguin Random House LLC
23 24 25 26 10 9 8 7 6 5 4 3 2 1
001–334116-Sept/2023

All rights reserved.
Without limiting the rights under the copyright reserved above, no part of this publication may be reproduced, stored in or introduced into a retrieval system, or transmitted, in any form, or by any means (electronic, mechanical, photocopying, recording, or otherwise), without the prior written permission of the copyright owner.
Published in Great Britain by Dorling Kindersley Limited

A catalog record for this book
is available from the Library of Congress.
HC ISBN: 978-0-7440-7539-7
PB ISBN: 978-0-7440-7540-3

DK books are available at special discounts when purchased in bulk for sales promotions, premiums, fundraising, or educational use. For details, contact: DK Publishing Special Markets,
1745 Broadway, 20th Floor, New York, NY 10019
SpecialSales@dk.com

Printed and bound in China

The publisher would like to thank the following for their kind permission to reproduce their images:
a=above; c=center; b=below; l=left; r=right; t=top; b/g=background

123RF.com: 1xpert 7bc, Dan Talson 38tr, Yasonya 15tr; **Alamy Stock Photo:** Rieger Bertrand / Hemis.fr 22-23b, Imaginechina Limited 1cb, Iain Masterton 33tl, Reuters / Gene Blevins 28tl, ZUMA Press, Inc. / Matthias Oesterle 42-43t; **Dorling Kindersley:** NASA 40tl; **Dreamstime.com:** 3000ad 3cb, 30-31b, Alankar2 26cla, Albertshakirov 36tl, Algol 32br, Aaron Amat 11bl, Abhijith Ar 37cr, Beats1 11t, BiancoBlue 16tl, Pavel Chagochkin 4-5, Denisismagilov 8clb, Dinozzaver 14-15b, Dml5050 42bl, Ecophoto 13tr, Ekkasit919 18tl, 43br, 45tr, Ryan Fletcher 27br, Libux77 20b, Malpetr 26-27t, Juan Moyano 30tl, Nexusplexus 39b, Sarawuth Pamoon 17tl, Gary Parker 21crb, Phartisan 26clb, Akarat Phasura 25tr, Simone Pitrolo 20tl, Plej92 30clb, Alexei Poselenov 9cra, Rawpixelimages 12tl, Piti Sirisiro 26tl, Joe Sohm 33crb, Sompong Sriphet 36b, Vladimir Stani¡i 44-45b, Lawrence W Stolte 34clb, Ievgenii Tryfonov 6, Vladischern 14tl, Rainer Zapka 7tr, Zstockphotos 34-35t; **Getty Images:** AFP / Staff / Yoshikazu Tsuno 40br, Corbis Historical / Photo Josse / Leemage 37bc, DigitalVision / John M Lund Photography Inc 41crb, Hulton Archive / Fototeca Storica Nazionale 8tl, Moment / Athima Tongloom 31tr, Stone / Kelvin Murray 8-9t, The Image Bank / Ashley Cooper 21tl, The Image Bank / P A Thompson 34tr, Sepia Times / Universal Images Group 44tl; **Getty Images / iStock:** E+ / ASKA 41t, E+ / Edwin Tan 12-13b, E+ / mladn61 24t, E+ / onurodemiz 13clb, 19, PonyWang 38tl, sarawuth702 16br, simon2579 10b, spawns 23cra; **NASA:** JSC 29tr; **Shutterstock.com:** metamorworks 22br, sicegame 28br

Cover images: Front: **Shutterstock.com:** Marko Aliaksandr cb, ART STOCK CREATIVE;
Back: **Shutterstock.com:** Andy Dean Photography bl, Chesky cra

All other images © Dorling Kindersley
For more information see: www.dkimages.com

For the curious
www.dk.com

Level 4

The Future

Rose Davidson

CONTENTS

7	Seeing the Future
10	The Future of Food
18	Future Homes
24	The Future of Travel
30	Future Cities

38 The Future of Fun
46 Glossary
47 Index
48 Quiz

SEEING THE FUTURE

Bzzzz! Your alarm goes off. You roll out of bed, walk over to the window, and wave hello to Earth. From here, the planet looks like a marble suspended among a sea of stars.

The year is 2070, and you're on board the latest space hotel, surrounded by other out-of-this-world guests. Some of them are more than 110 years old! You all head to the hotel's restaurants for some breakfast, made with ingredients grown on the space station.

Believe it or not, this might be your future vacation. What else could the future have in store for you? And how can you know?

Orbital Vacations
Space hotels of the future would always be on the move. They would travel on a circular path around Earth, giving guests a constant view of the planet.

When viewed from space, Earth's blue waters, green landscapes, and white clouds combine to look like a swirly marble.

Blast from the Past
In 1909, Italian poet Filippo Tommaso Marinetti coined the term "futurism." It began as an artistic movement that celebrated innovation and change.

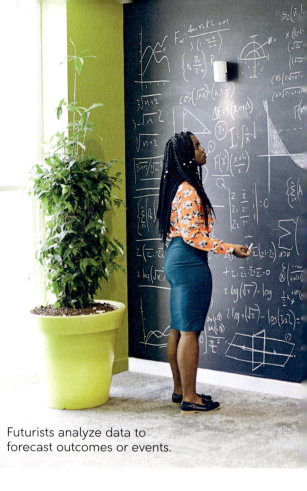

Futurists analyze data to forecast outcomes or events.

Future Fields
Futurists can apply their predictions to many different fields, from music or fashion to health or food.

While it's impossible to actually see the future, some scientists—called futurists—can make educated guesses. They gather data from the past and present to find trends. Then, they analyze the trends to predict what's most likely to happen next. Often, the things they identify require advanced technology. That means they may not be affordable to everyone, at least not at first.

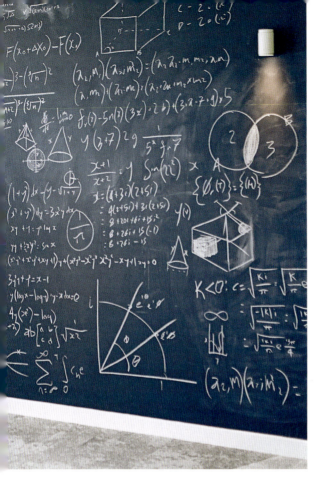

Living Longer
Today, the global average life expectancy is 73 years. In 1970, people only lived for 56 years on average. Fifty years from now, futurists predict the average life span could be more than 100 years!

The guesses that a futurist makes are called forecasts. Similar to a meteorologist predicting rain or snow in the week ahead, a futurist's forecast predicts a specific outcome or event in the future.

Sometimes, these forecasts come true. Other times, they're a total bust. But it's fun to guess! Read on to find out about some of the exciting things that might exist in the future.

THE FUTURE OF FOOD

In the years ahead, futurists predict we'll have more food choices than ever before. Food might be packed with new, never-before-tasted flavors. Customized foods might even be made based on your body's unique makeup, so doctors could prescribe meals for patients with special dietary needs.

The Science of Eating
Nutrigenomics is the study of how our bodies respond to what we eat and drink.

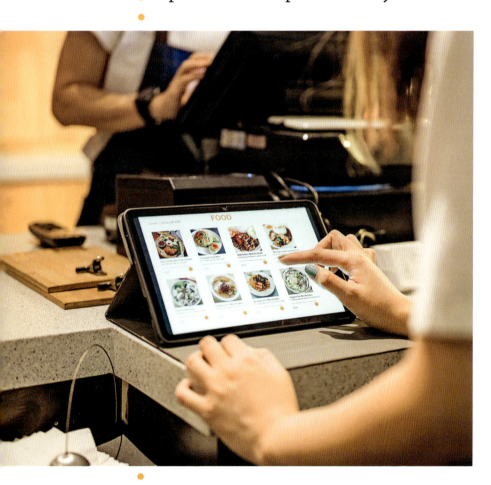

Just like today, what and how we eat in the future will be driven by the culture around us. Thanks to social media, people could have more and more real-time insight into what other people do and don't like to eat, influencing the choices we all make.

Tasty Tubes
The ways we taste foods are expanding, too. In 2020, researchers in Japan created a device that people could lick to virtually taste foods. When licked, the five tubes in the device recreate taste sensations based on the five different types of tastes: sour, sweet, salty, bitter, and a meaty flavor called umami.

World Population
In 1970, there were roughly 3.7 billion people on Earth. By 2022, that number had risen to 8 billion. By 2070, it's estimated that 9.2 billion people will populate the planet.

The choices we have will be affected by two major issues: a growing population and a changing climate. Both issues will impact how we grow our food.

As the global population rises, people will need more space. This means there will be less land available to grow crops and raise livestock. One solution, especially for foods like fruits and vegetables, is to grow up … literally!

12

In some parts of the world, tall buildings with multiple floors of produce already stretch toward the sky. These "vertical farms" could become more popular in urban areas, where the food would be accessible to more people.

Instead of people harvesting the food when it's ready, robots might step in to help. Automated robots could collect the produce from the building, sort it, clean it, and deliver it for people to eat.

Room to Roam
Today, more than a fourth of the world's land is used to produce livestock, such as chickens and cows. That's more land than is used to grow all of the world's forests combined.

Friendly Farms
Some futurists think high-rise buildings could become their own kind of cities, with each building's farm supporting all of its residents.

Warming Up
An atmosphere is a band of gas around a planet. Carbon dioxide is a greenhouse gas that traps heat in Earth's atmosphere. When heat is trapped, temperatures on Earth begin to rise.

Climate change is a long-term change in Earth's climate patterns. This shift will likely put more pressure on our food systems, or the ways we make food. Rising temperatures could affect which foods we eat and where they are raised or grown.

Climate change alters precipitation patterns, causing floods or droughts. It also alters temperature patterns, which could someday make it impossible for farmers to grow crops they have traditionally grown in a region. With those changes, farmers may see pests and weeds that have never been a problem in their area before.

For farmers who raise animals for food, production could decline without enough water or feed grains.

Some scientists think an unlikely alternative could help: algae. These aquatic plants are packed with protein that would provide nutrition. Algae also need carbon to grow. As they grow, the plants help the air by taking in carbon dioxide, a gas that contributes to climate change.

Algae farms could one day replace other kinds of farms. And the algae produced could serve as a substitute for meats in beef patties and other products. Protein-rich bugs might be listed on the menu, too!

Food Insecurity
People sometimes have difficulty accessing enough nutritious food—usually due to high prices or low supply. This situation is called food insecurity.

Problem Solved
Artificial intelligence uses computers to combine data and perform tasks that humans would normally do. This includes things like translating languages or solving mathematical equations.

In restaurants, robotic kitchen assistants could help prep food and deliver it to tables. Artificial intelligence could analyze data about these dishes and help create new crowd-pleasing recipes. And instead of a menu, 3D glasses might show a tasty dish in front of you, helping you select your meal. Floating next to each menu item, you might also see social media comments from people who have recently tried the meal.

If you prefer takeout over dining in, you might see changes, too. As drones replace delivery drivers, you may spot your dinner soaring through the sky in an enclosed box. Drones carrying lighter items might be made with natural materials, such as fungus. That might sound kind of gross, but it would be good for the environment. If the drone got stuck somewhere, parts of it would break down into soil. It wouldn't be litter for long.

Hot Dog, Anyone? Drones are already used to record and broadcast sporting events. And now, they're being deployed for food delivery inside arenas, too. After an attendee places an order for a stadium snack, a drone drops off the order to the hungry fan in the stands.

Virtual Fits
Instead of shopping for clothes by size, one day you could have clothes that were designed on your own digital avatar using your exact measurements. One fashion designer is already making clothes this way, with the hope of reducing the amount of poor-fitting clothes that end up in landfills.

FUTURE HOMES

Imagine finishing your school day and having no chores to do. Futurists predict that, with the help of robots, we're headed that way. "Smart" homes will assist us with more daily tasks, such as heating up leftovers on the stove or shopping for groceries to restock the fridge. They could also conserve more energy and continuously adapt to changes in the outside environment.

What's in the closet of your future home? Your clothes might come with built-in sensors to track your temperature. If you were too warm, the sensors might detect if you had a fever. They might also monitor your heart rate. They would send this information to your doctor via Wi-Fi to the cloud.

Made to Order
Robot chefs can now cook up entire meals—and in the future, they might be as common as refrigerators. Among their skills, these household chefs can turn on ovens, pick up pans and utensils, and stir and flip ingredients. Bring on the pancakes!

Early Floating Homes
For roughly 4,000 years, the Uros people in South America have lived in a small village on Lake Titicaca. They weave rafts out of reeds and build their homes on top.

In the future, you might not play catch in the front yard—but you might be able to swim! And instead of hopping in the car to get to school, you might jump into a canoe and paddle. Platforms with schools or parks would sit on top of the water, providing common spaces for community members to gather.

That's life in a floating city. Some countries, such as the Netherlands, have already built floating cities in response to floods and housing shortages. These floating homes are protected against extreme weather such as hurricanes and heavy rain.

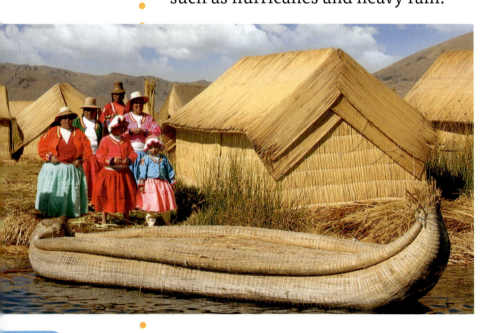

In some places, shock-absorbing materials in the buildings reduce the sway from being on water. Poles keep the homes anchored to the shore.

As climate change causes oceans to rise, this kind of living could become more mainstream. By 2050, water levels along the US coastline are estimated to rise as much as 12 inches (30.5 cm). That might not sound like a lot, but it's enough to put hundreds of thousands of homes at risk of flooding.

City on the Sea
A floating city designed as a prototype in Busan, South Korea, could one day grow to house more than 100,000 people along the coast. The city's foundation will rise as sea levels rise. The floating community is a model for a new type of city that could withstand severe storms of the future.

Dynamic Designs
Architects have dreamed up designs of future floating homes that are shaped like aquatic objects such as icebergs and jellyfish.

Life might get wetter for some people in the future, but it could get sunnier for others. To take advantage of all that sunlight, some future homes could be built on rotating platforms. Similar to how a carousel spins—but much slower—these homes would move in a single, complete circle each day. This would give solar panels on their roofs maximum exposure to sunlight as the Sun moves through the sky during the day.

Follow the Sun
Rotating homes designed by architects in Portugal were inspired by sunflowers. Sunflowers turn their heads from east to west each day to follow the Sun as it moves through the sky.

The Heliotrope, a building in Freiburg, Germany, rotates throughout the day to follow the Sun.

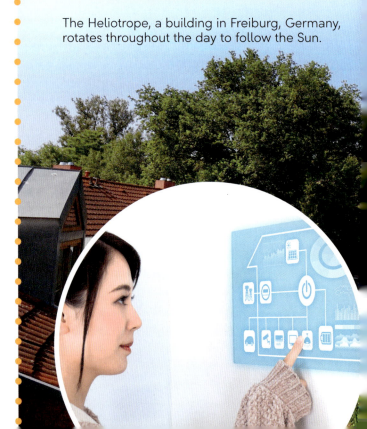

22

Energy captured by the solar panels would be used to power dishwashers, refrigerators, and other appliances inside the home. A rotating home would not only lower energy bills but would also give people ever-changing views from their windows!

Sun Power
When sunlight hits a solar panel, cells inside the panel absorb the light's energy. The energy then creates electrical charges that move, causing electricity to flow.

A Slow Transition
Instead of suddenly filling the streets with self-driving cars, carmakers are slowly introducing the new technology. Each year, cars could have more automatic features, until drivers are no longer needed at all.

THE FUTURE OF TRAVEL

It's impossible to think about the future and not dream about the possibilities for travel. Oh, the wonderful places we could go, zipping to the edge of the universe in our warp-speed spaceships. At least that's what they show in the movies.

Here on Earth, there are more practical things to deal with, like everyday transportation. In the near future, that means cars.

While only a relatively small number of self-driving cars are on the streets today, futurists agree that self-driving cars could soon be the norm. Most likely, they would run on electricity. Sensors would make them aware of their surroundings. They would use Wi-Fi to connect with other vehicles. These features would help them safely navigate the roads. And being electric, they would be good for the environment, too.

For those who feel like getting some air, flying taxis could be the way to get from Point A to Point B. Unlike helicopters, the taxis would be electric-powered, making for a much quieter ride. Futurists predict that these rides could be even more affordable than some of today's taxi rides. But before we take off, government officials will have to work together to create new traffic laws for the sky.

Car Ownership
Cars spend most of their time parked in driveways and parking lots. So, privately owned cars may become a thing of the past. Instead, people may travel in fleets of self-driving electric vehicles.

First of Its Kind
The first model for a self-driving car, presented at the 1939 World's Fair, was a radio-controlled vehicle guided by magnetic spikes along a roadway.

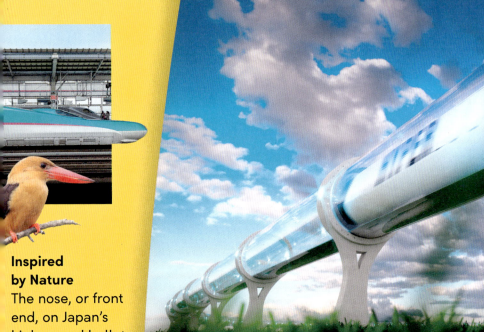

Inspired by Nature
The nose, or front end, on Japan's high-speed bullet trains was inspired by the pointed beak of the kingfisher, a type of bird.

Burning Up
Some commercial jets burn a gallon of fuel per second. That's 3,600 gallons (13,600 liters) of fuel per hour.

Today's airplanes are powered by fuel and fly thousands of feet above the ground. Airplanes of the future might function more like cars. They might have small, quiet, electric motors and fly lower in the sky, closer to where people live and work. They may take off and land vertically, making it easy to quickly pick up and drop off passengers. They would essentially become taxis, transporting people on a daily basis.

On the ground, imagine a vehicle that turns a six-hour nonstop drive into a quick 30-minute trip. That's exactly what trains of the future could do.

Just like today's trains, high-speed train systems could carry people or goods across long distances. But in the future, we might travel on a hyperloop. Pods filled with passengers or cargo could whiz through tubes at up to 750 miles per hour (1,200 kph)! The pods would levitate on magnets as they zip through a tube. The reduced drag would create a safe ride.

A Cleaner Flight
Today's airplanes release greenhouse gases, such as nitrogen oxide, that contribute to climate change. By using electric energy for some functions, hybrid-electric airplanes could eliminate up to 95 percent of the dangerous gases released during flight.

New Space Race
In 2021, two privately owned companies made history by launching their first passenger flights into space. The trips were only nine days apart!

Advances in transportation won't be limited to Earth. Space travel has already taken off, rocketing people past Earth's atmosphere and back. A few people have already taken short trips into space. But the tickets cost millions of dollars. And during takeoff, the rockets released hundreds of tons of harmful gases into the atmosphere. As larger spacecraft and new technologies are developed in the future, spaceflight could become cleaner and affordable to more people.

Going Up!
The idea for a space elevator was first described by rocket scientist Konstantin Tsiolkovsky in 1895.

28

For longer journeys, you might hop on a special space elevator instead. If developed, this new transportation system would carry people past Earth's atmosphere along a superstrong cable. The elevator would offer a cheaper, more energy-efficient way to send people and materials to space. But it probably wouldn't be fast—a one-way trip would take days or weeks. But, from the elevator's drop-off point, you might one day be able to connect with another spacecraft going to the Moon or Mars!

If you'd like to stay a while, you could book a room in a space hotel, fully equipped with low-gravity basketball courts, stellar views, and an outdoor space walk. The hotels would orbit Earth and constantly spin to create a sense of artificial gravity. So, inside most parts of these hotels, you would feel like you were back home on Earth.

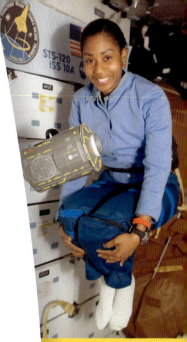

Change in Gravity
While common areas inside space hotels would mimic the gravity on Earth, other areas would be reserved for the full space experience. Pressurized rooms with microgravity, which is a low-gravity atmosphere, would allow visitors to spin and float like an astronaut.

Superblocks
In Barcelona, Spain, cars have been banned in certain parts of the city to create more walkable public spaces called "superblocks." This idea could become the norm for other cities in the future.

Green Roofs
A green roof is a layer of vegetation that's planted on top of a building.

FUTURE CITIES

Before COVID-19 began spreading across the globe in 2020, the number of people living in cities had been rising for decades. Remote work allowed some people to move away from expensive cities. But people will likely move back to these areas in the decades to come. As much as two-thirds of all people could be living in cities by the year 2050.

What will these cities look like? For starters, imagine more green spaces. You might find mini-parks inside libraries or apartment buildings. "Green" roofs could be covered with gardens, fruit trees, and native plants that attract wildlife such as birds and bees. These animals would be welcome visitors, as they would spread pollen to help new plants grow.

Step on It! An innovative type of pavement made from recycled rubber was introduced at the 2012 Olympic Games. As visitors walked on it, the pavement harvested energy from the impact of their footsteps. It converted that energy into electricity used to power lights. In the future, this type of pavement may be on roads and sidewalks all around the world.

31

Going Green
The first algae-powered building was constructed in Hamburg, Germany, in 2013. The Sun causes algae to grow and provide shade, and the building absorbs the Sun's heat to warm its hot water supply.

Fossil Fuels
Fossil fuels are natural resources, such as coal, oil, or natural gas. Unlike water or wind, fossil fuels are nonrenewable, or unable to be replaced.

Imagine the Sun rising over the skyline, emitting an orange glow through the clouds. The sunlight falls on roofs across the city. Some roofs are flourishing with plants, and others are dotted with landing pads for flying taxis and drones. The rest are carefully covered with solar panels.

Today, cities already use some renewable resources, such as wind and solar power, to generate electricity. But they still use fossil fuels to produce the rest of their power. Fossil fuels are limited, so once we use them all up, they're gone. They also cause pollution, which raises global temperatures and leads to climate change.

A Model City
Masdar, a city in a desert in the United Arab Emirates, was built to rely solely on renewable energy. The city was designed to advance the development of energy and technology that could be used in sustainable cities around the world.

Cities of the future would have ways to battle those problems. Many cities could be powered purely by renewable resources. The glass panels in buildings' windows could be filled with molecules made up of living algae that absorb air pollutants and improve air quality while reducing the need for energy.

Using artificial intelligence to track energy use, smart buildings could learn to regulate heating systems. They might alert building managers about high usage, so the buildings can use their energy most efficiently.

Renewable Resources
Renewable resources are natural resources that can be replaced, such as solar, water, or wind.

33

Skip the Salt
The process of removing salt from water is called desalination.

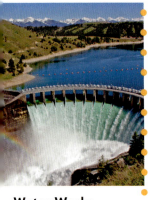

Water Works
When water is used for energy, it is called hydropower.

What about water? People consume water in lots of ways. They drink it, bathe in it, play in it, and use it to clean themselves and their surroundings. People also use water to generate energy.

In future decades water shortages will be more widespread. People cannot survive without water, so additional sources must be found. Some scientists are already working on ways to make ocean water drinkable. But that requires removing salt from the water. This is a very expensive process and could harm ocean habitats.

34

A more direct solution would be collecting rainwater from rooftops. Once filtered, rainwater could be stored and used as drinkable water. This could be especially helpful in parts of the world where water shortages have become more common, or where the existing water is unsafe to drink.

In cities, massive rainwater collection systems could be installed on tops of buildings and funneled down to each building for people to use. With systems like these, people could replenish their water supply each time it rained.

Saving the Rain
In the future, many homes might have built-in rainwater collection systems.

Robotic Limbs
Prosthetics replace missing or injured body parts. Using sensors that read messages from the wearer's brain, robotic prosthetics move like a part of the person's body.

Health care could also change a lot in the future. Inside some hospitals, robots might be on call to help care for sick patients. Already, there are robots that bring medicines, run tests, and assist surgeons in operating rooms with a wide variety of procedures. Where available, future robots could take over even more tasks in hospitals so doctors and nurses have more time to spend with their patients.

Not everyone has access to a hospital. Some people who do are unable to make the trip. As technologies to detect and treat diseases become more advanced, more people may be able to get treatment in their doctor's office or at home. Someday, personal health robots may even alert people to possible health problems, giving them an early warning so they seek help when needed.

At the doctor's office, a physician could offer customized medicines to treat illnesses. By studying a person's genes, a doctor would be able to predict and proactively treat health problems before they start. The medicines patients receive might be uniquely made based on their genetic makeup. In addition to helping patients recover, these medicines could also reduce side effects, such as headaches or fatigue.

Nostradamus

Destroying Diseases
As scientists and physicians continue to study genes, they could learn how to change them. The genes that carry some diseases, such as cancers or heart disease, could be altered or "turned off."

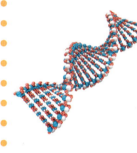

Predicting a Pandemic
Famous for being a supposed "seer" of the future, Nostradamus was a French astrologer who made predictions about major historical events, including the COVID-19 pandemic.

Bluetooth
The name for the wireless technology "Bluetooth" comes from a 10th-century king of Denmark. Famous for uniting parts of Scandinavia, he also had a damaged tooth that was blue.

AI Music
Artificial intelligence is changing the music industry. AI can now be used to write songs and lyrics. It can also duplicate voices, recreating performances by your favorite artists.

THE FUTURE OF FUN

According to futurists, concerts with your favorite musicians could become more interactive in the coming years. Do you want to tell your favorite musician how much you admire them, or do you want to request your favorite song? Open chat rooms during live shows could allow you to communicate with your pop idols while they're on stage.

In the sports arena, you could have access to a personalized video feed to follow your favorite players. Friends from social media may appear on a stadium map so you can snag a nearby seat. Feeling hungry? Walk to a food kiosk and wait for a robot to serve you a meal. When you exit the stadium, virtual reality rides could give you a chance to view game clips from the players' perspectives.

Predicting the Future?
Science fiction books, TV shows, and movies often seem to predict the future. For example, technology like Bluetooth, touch screen monitors, and voice activation appeared in *Star Trek* films long before they were invented.

Suit Up!
Specialized suits could be another new experience to show up in amusement parks. The suits would use hydraulic pressure to mimic microgravity. Parkgoers wearing the suits would feel what it's like to be an astronaut in space.

Second Skin
Electronic skins already exist, though they are used for medical purposes rather than entertainment. Sensors in the electronic skin shown here monitor a person's vital signs, including heart rate, body temperature, and blood pressure.

Someday, when you enter a theme park, you could be supplied with superpowers. Well, not literally. But it might feel pretty close!

Wearable electronics could help parkgoers tap into superhuman senses. As you enter the park, this super-tiny tech could be printed onto your hand or arm like a second skin. While you explore, it could record your physical experiences and send nerve signals to and from your friends. You will be able to feel what your friends feel—almost as if you've traded bodies.

You might even be able to control rides with your mind. Sensors connected to your body could detect your thoughts, which would be transmitted to an object that you could control. You could battle it out in a 3D spaceship, or go on a safari and feel like you were one of the animals. The places you could go are endless—and mind-blowing!

Mind Your Health
In the future, reading minds won't be just for fun. The ability to read minds could also help medical professionals treat neurological and mental illnesses.

Virtual Reality
Virtual reality (VR) is technology that shows you a different place entirely, usually through a headset. A video game where players feel like they're actually driving is an example of virtual reality.

How will we watch movies? Closer than ever! New developments in augmented reality could bring 3D images of actors off the screen and into your living room. Virtual reality technology used in video games, including the ability to interact with objects and perform specific actions, could also show up on the big screen.

Augmented Reality

Augmented reality (AR) is technology that layers images over what you see in real life. A camera filter that overlays a silly hat on your selfie is an example of augmented reality.

At the movies, the stars on the screen will probably still look like the celebrities you know, but one of them might actually be you! Face-recognition technology could be used to identify and replace the images of famous actors, allowing you to step into the actor's shoes and act in their place.

43

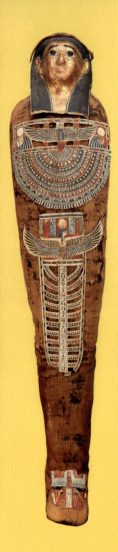

At museums, you can now come face-to-face with the past. Holograms, a form of mixed reality, can bring ancient people, places, and things "back to life" through a headset. Dinosaurs can reappear, showing us how they once lived and moved. People from the past can "visit" the present day and have a conversation with guests.

Mummy Moves The Reading Public Museum in Pennsylvania once developed a hologram experience that portrayed a mummy speaking to guests.

In the future, holograms might even bring the ancient world to your fingertips. With new technologies, you might be able to feel a dinosaur's skin or run your fingers over the lid of a mummy's sarcophagus. Instead of traveling to a museum, these holograms might come directly to you in your home. The future is full of exciting possibilities!

Mixing It Up
"Mixed reality" is when real and virtual worlds overlap. It allows physical and digital items to exist in the same physical space.

45

GLOSSARY

Analyze
To examine something for the purposes of explanation and interpretation

Artificial intelligence
The use of computers to combine data and perform tasks that humans would normally do

Augmented reality
Technology that layers images over what you see in real life

Climate change
A long-term change in Earth's climate patterns

Drag
A force exerted by air or liquid that slows down a moving object

Drone
A small, pilotless aircraft flown over land or water

Forecast
A prediction or estimate of a future event

Futurist
A scientist who gathers data from the past and present to find trends to predict what's most likely to happen in the future

Hologram
A 3D image made with a photo projection

Hybrid
Something made by combining two things

Hyperloop
A high-speed transportation system that moves people in a hovering pod

Mixed reality
A combination of physical and digital items that exist in the same physical space

Self-sustaining
Able to continue without assistance from outside forces

Superblock
A large commercial or residential block where cars are not allowed

Trend
A general direction in which something is growing or changing

Virtual reality
Technology that shows viewers a different place entirely, usually through a headset

INDEX

airplanes 26, 27
algae farms 15
algae-powered buildings 32, 33
amusement parks 40–41
artificial intelligence 16, 33, 38
augmented reality (AR) 42, 43
Barcelona, Spain 30
Bluetooth technology 38
bullet trains 26
Busan, South Korea 21
carbon dioxide 14, 15
cars
    bans on 30
    self-driving 24–25
cities 30–37
    floating 20–21
    "green" roofs 30, 31–32
    health care 36–37
    renewable energy 32–33
    superblocks 30
    water use 34–35
climate change
    flooding homes 21
    from fossil fuels 32
    from greenhouse gases 27
    impact on farms 12, 14–15
clothes 18
COVID-19 pandemic 37
desalination 34
drones 17, 32
Earth, from space 7
farms 12–15
floating homes 20–21

flying taxis 25, 32
food 10–17
    customized 10
    delivery 17
    growing 12–15
    restaurants 16–17
    robot chefs 16, 19
    tasting 11
food insecurity 15
forecasts 9
fossil fuels 32
fun 38–45
futurists 8–9
gravity 29
"green" roofs 30, 31–32
greenhouse gases 14, 27
health care 36–37, 40, 41
Heliotrope 22
holograms 44–45
homes 18–23
    clothes 18
    floating 20–21
    robot chefs 19
    rotating 22–23
hydropower 34
hyperloop 27
life expectancy 9
Marinetti, Filippo Tommaso 8
Masdar, United Arab Emirates 33
microgravity 29, 40
mixed reality 44
movies 42–43
museums 44–45
music 38
Nostradamus 37
nutrigenomics 10
pandemics 37

pavement, harvesting energy 31
population 12
prosthetics 36
rainwater collection systems 35
renewable energy 32–33
restaurants 16–17
robots
    food service 16, 19, 39
    harvesting food 13
    for health care 36–37
    in homes 18, 19
rotating homes 22–23
self-driving cars 24–25
skin, electronic 40
"smart" buildings 33
"smart" homes 18
solar panels 22–23, 32
space elevator 28, 29
space hotels 7, 29
space travel 7, 28–29
sports 39
sunflowers 22
superblocks 30
taxis, flying 25, 32
theme parks 40–41
trains 26, 27
travel 24–29
    airplanes 26, 27
    cars 24–25
    space travel 28–29
    trains 26, 27
Tsiolkovsky, Konstantin 28
Uros people 20
virtual reality (VR) 39, 42
water resources 34–35
wearable electronics 40

QUIZ

Answer the questions to see what you have learned. Check your answers in the key below.

1. What kind of scientist makes predictions about the future?
2. What natural material might be used to make drones in the future?
3. What do you call the long-term change in Earth's climate patterns?
4. Which plant inspired the design of rotating homes that would follow the Sun?
5. In the future, what could transport goods or people at speeds up to 750 miles per hour (1,200 kph)?
6. What might you find on a "green" roof?
7. True or False: Someday, doctors may be able to alter or turn off genes that cause diseases.
8. What is a hologram?

1. A futurist 2. Fungus 3. Climate change 4. The sunflower
5. A hyperloop 6. Gardens, fruit trees, and native plants 7. True
8. A 3D image made with a photo projection